MW01626016

The Paper Butterfly

Ona Kingdon

Emotive Expressions

First Edition

Contents

This book is dedicated to all who plant milkweed and other pollinator friendly plants in their gardens; to the Monarch Watch organization and the people who take the time to tag monarch butterflies; to municipalities, businesses, farmers and individuals who preserve land and plant native species that enrich our natural habitats; to Michael G. LaFosse, an amazing master in origami; and to each one of you for reading this book and taking an interest in finding out more about monarchs.

Thank you!

Metamorphosis

Chapter 1

The long, graceful fingers moved, turned, and folded in an enchantingly rhythmic dance. As her Maker skillfully formed the creases of her body, the paper butterfly sensed such tenderness and compassion. Every soft caress of his fingers filled her soul with his warmth.

She felt herself sway first to the left, then to the right, as the fingers began to form the pleats of her wings. Suddenly, the paper butterfly sensed a flutter deep within her folds. It almost seemed as if this feeling would carry her high into the air. But the sensation was fleeting, and as she lay in her Maker's hands waiting for the dance to continue, she longed to experience that sensation again.

The turning and creasing began once more and after a few more folds, the paper butterfly felt complete. She moved her small head to look more carefully at how she had been formed.

She felt sure that her Maker had designed her to be beautiful, but she also wondered if there was a deeper reason why he created her. She hoped that her life would hold more meaning than simply being an object of beauty, but as a newly formed butterfly, she had no idea what her purpose might be.

Jolted from her thoughts by the awareness that she was moving again, the paper butterfly trembled as she felt a waft of cool air flow over her wings. She longed to nuzzle once more into the warmth of her Maker's hands but felt them slowly slipping away.

Placed on a long slender twig, the paper butterfly watched as a clear, cocoon-like object was placed over her. She sensed that this barrier was meant to protect her, but the physical separation from her Maker tugged at her heart. His hands lingered for a while, then faded away into the unknown.

The paper butterfly was alone.

She had no real idea how long she spent in her cocoon. Days seemed to pass in a haze of images that danced across the horizon. There were moments when fiery colours tumbled down like confetti, coating everything below in a carpet of scarlet, golden yellow, and flaming orange. As the paper butterfly watched them, she longed to fly with the strange swirling creatures.

Then there were times when feathery fingers covered everything in an icy sheen, and tiny, intricately crafted, white flakes seemed to swirl around the sky, chasing each other in a playful game.

"Your dance is so enchanting," she would sigh dreamily.

Months passed, and the accumulating layers of dust on the outer surface of her cocoon made it feel increasingly claustrophobic. Shadows of light and dark were all that the paper butterfly's eyes could now detect. She could distinguish day from night, and where the window to the outside world lay, but nothing more.

Without colour in her world, the paper butterfly felt sad.

"Killy-klee!"

The shrill cry pierced through her thoughts as a shadow moved swiftly across the surface of her cocoon.

"I wonder who you are," pondered the paper butterfly.

She closed her eyes to help visualize this majestic soul more clearly.

"Killy-klee, killy-klee!" it screeched again.

The paper butterfly pictured a magnificent creature with outstretched wings racing across the sky, chasing the setting sun as it journeyed beneath the horizon.

"Thank you for reminding me that I am not alone," she replied.

Sound became the paper butterfly's connection to the world beyond and a way to pass the time each day. When the light in her cocoon was at its brightest, she would listen to the song of a playful soul who seemed to tease her with his calls.

"Chick-a-dee-dee-dee, come and fly with me!" he would sing excitedly.

"Oh, I wish," echoed the paper butterfly longingly.

Later, as the light began to dim, she would hear the gentle calls of creatures softly whispering secrets to each other. She pictured them tenderly nuzzling together, taking comfort in each other's warmth. Then, as the light faded, she would listen to them flapping their wings and couldn't help but flutter her own, too.

"Oh, take me with you," she would cry.

One morning, just as the faintest glow of light began to cast dim shadows onto the surface of her very grimy cocoon, a new song filled the air. It felt so close that the paper butterfly was sure the creature was singing just for her.

"Pui, Pui Pui," it called.

"Well, hello to you, too," the paper butterfly answered politely. "I am so pleased to meet you."

To her delight, the creature replied again.

"Pui, Pui."

"Your melody warms my lonely soul as much as any ray of sunshine!" the paper butterfly exclaimed. "It reminds me of the golden leaves when they were blown around by the breeze. I wonder if you glow in the sunshine as they do."

The sound stopped.

"Oh, please sing to me again," the paper butterfly begged.

Spilling notes of molten sweetness filled the air once more. Then, to the paper butterfly's absolute delight, a second voice joined in. The duet was as soulful as a flute and as tender as the touch of her Maker's gentle hands against her newly formed wings.

She closed her eyes to try to picture these magical creatures more clearly.

Suddenly, their song changed.

"Here, here! Come right here, my dear," they both trilled.

What had triggered this? Was it something they had seen, or were they simply teasing her? How the paper butterfly wished she could see what was happening.

Almost at once, she felt a gentle breeze flow across her wings, and the softness of her Maker's hands tenderly lifting her.

With a gasp, the paper butterfly opened her eyes. Everything around her was so bright and clear; the colours more vibrant, the sounds more dynamic. Without the cocoon enclosing her, she felt truly alive.

She was placed on a beautiful flower next to an open window. A sweet heavenly scent filled the air and the paper butterfly felt a wave of peaceful tranquility wash over her.

As the sun's rays poured in, they gave the petals surrounding her their gift of light. The flower thanked them by glowing even brighter. The paper butterfly eagerly caressed the petal's silky softness.

Suddenly, a gust of wind caught her wings, and she was lifted out of the open window. Tumbling, spinning, whirling, and swirling, she fought hard to steady her beating heart. Then slowly, but with increasing strength, she began to move her wings in time to life's rhythm.

"Oh my, I can fly! I can REALLY fly!" she cried excitedly as the warm wind whistled over her paper wings.

The fresh new growth of spring raced past her, leaving behind contrails of colour. Above, a pair of majestic creatures with long black necks chattered noisily as they flew. They alternated their calls so rapidly that it seemed like only one of them was talking.

"Come on, come on, come on," they honked.

They joined a few others and formed an arrowhead in the sky to show the paper butterfly the direction she should take. Each bird flew slightly above and behind the bird in front and took turns leading the way.

The paper butterfly followed.

Chapter 2

They guided her to an idyllic spot on the banks of a stream where swirls of blue artistically wove their way through the landscape. A subtle, powdery scent filled the air, and hundreds of fuzzy insects with small, stubby wings buzzed around enthusiastically. Full of curiosity, the paper butterfly fluttered down to join them.

She marvelled at the majestic beauty of the wild blue blooms standing tall above the glistening water. Their velvety smooth down-turned sepals provided her with a safe place to land, and the delicately painted veins of white, blue, and gold acted as runway markers guiding her into the depths of the flower.

The paper butterfly felt honoured to have been given the privilege of exploring such a sacred space. It felt strangely intimate, silky soft, and such a stark contrast to the showy beauty of the outer petals. If only she knew why the flower wished her to be there.

She squeezed in further to see if she could find the answer to her question and felt part of the bloom brush against her body.

Suddenly, a cloud of pollen dust fell around her and the paper butterfly sneezed.

"Oh my!" she exclaimed.

She pulled herself back from the flower's centre and looked around. Millions of tiny particles coated everything. Even her own body was encased in the strange powdery substance.

"Just look at all these dusty tears," she cried, bowing her small head in shame. "I am so sorry. You have shown me nothing but kindness and now I have made you weep."

"Do not fret. You didn’t wound or injure the flower," called a nearby voice. "The dusty tears you speak of are not drops of sadness, but extremely important grains of pollen!"

Talking to her was a creature almost half her size, with a slender body and wings that were the deepest silver-blue fringed with a ribbon of pure white.

"See, over here is the stamen," he said, flying closer and pointing enthusiastically with his antennae as he spoke.

"And of course, you are already familiar with the anther over there..."

"Excuse me, but who are you?" asked the paper butterfly, quite bewildered by this strangely enthusiastic creature.

"Oh, right...sorry," apologized the small blue butterfly, "I completely forgot to introduce myself. I am a Karner Blue. Are you, by any chance, a newly eclosed butterfly?"

Having someone as beautiful and as knowledgeable as this creature take an interest in her made the paper butterfly blush. She wasn't certain what he meant by the term 'eclosed', but hoped he was asking about her dance of creation.

Swooping and fluttering around him, she described the twists and turns of her Maker's hands as he had folded her body. Then spiralling upwards, she recounted the feeling of the very first flutter in her wings.

As she twirled back down, the grains of dust the flower had gifted her fell like confetti over everything around her.

"And that is how I became a paper butterfly," she concluded.

She landed with a ceremonial flutter.

The Karner Blue looked at her with great intrigue.

"I have observed many distinct species on my travels," he stated, "but you are the only one created from paper I have ever had the pleasure to meet. Your orange and black wings remind me of the magnificent monarchs. Are you a rare breed, too?"

"I am not sure," replied the paper butterfly. "I have yet to meet another like me, but I sense that maybe my creator made others."

"I wish I could locate another like me," responded the blue butterfly with a tremble in his voice.

He bowed his head and distractedly caressed the petals of the lupine beneath them.

"What's wrong?" the paper butterfly inquired.

The Karner Blue tried his best to explain.

"Our species depends on the sundial lupine; It is our host plant, the only thing our young can eat. It used to be plentiful, but the sandy-soiled habitats where it grows are now much harder to find. As a result, there is simply not enough lupine growing to support our young."

He stopped and looked directly at the paper butterfly.

"You see, every species depends upon the actions and presence of others around it to survive and flourish. No single thing can survive in isolation; No one species is more important than the other. A swathe of lupine like this is such a wonderful sight, but because many natural areas where it grows have been destroyed, our species is now also in decline."

A tear trickled down his face. He quickly wiped it away.

"I have been searching for days to find a female Karner Blue but have found none. I fear there might be no more in this area," he concluded.

The paper butterfly looked concerned.

"Don't give up," she pleaded. "If I see a female Karner Blue, I will tell her where to find you. I wish I could do more, but I am merely a paper butterfly and don't know how."

The Karner Blue was grateful for the paper butterfly's warm compassion as the air seemed to have adopted his sombre mood.

"You have already helped me immensely by being a listening ear to my troubles," he replied, "but if you would like to do more, go and find the wild blue lupine, collect the pollen on your wings and body, and then fly to another and rub the dust onto it. This helps the plant to reproduce."

Happy to be of help, the paper butterfly gracefully lifted herself into the air and glided over to a nearby bloom. She buried her head into the flower's centre until she could feel its loving caress on her back, and then hurriedly flew onto the next patch she could find.

As she continued to pollinate flower after flower she thought about what the small blue butterfly had taught her. The elements in our world are all connected, each species depends upon the actions and presence of others around it to survive and flourish.

"I wonder how I fit into this interconnected puzzle of life?" she mused.

Jolted from her thoughts by a sudden gust of wind, she hurriedly flew over to the branch of a nearby tree.

The sky above was filled with menacing clouds that seemed to have taken the sun prisoner behind their ominous grey cloak. As their damp shadows continued to roll towards her, the paper butterfly prayed that they would not not wrap their evil, wispy tentacles around her and take her hostage, too.

Tiny pearls of rain began to fall, and the paper butterfly shivered nervously. Each droplet that landed was so small, but together were enough to make the leaves around her lean dejectedly toward the earth and cry tears of sorrow onto the ground below.

The paper butterfly wished her knowledgeable friend, Karner Blue, was still close enough to reassure her, but she had flown far in her search for lupine and he was nowhere to be seen.

The rain intensified, and the increasingly angry droplets smacked against her fragile wings making them feel weak and heavy. Frightened, she tried to take flight once more, but her moisture-laden wings were now too damp and wrinkled to make this possible.

She wished with all her heart that she could somehow be transported back into the warm, comforting hands of her Maker, but wishing was not going to help her now. So, with her last ounce of strength, the paper butterfly dragged herself underneath one of the leaves in search of shelter.

Beneath the leaf was a different world. The noise of the rain splashing on the veins above her drummed in the paper butterfly's ears, but the cold bullets of rain could not touch her.

"Thank you for protecting me," she whispered gratefully.

She gazed up at the roof of green and traced its intricate veins with her antenna. Somehow they reminded her of the patterning on her creator's hands and she felt comfort in this thought. Closing her eyes, she let the rhythm of the leaf's gently swaying movement soothe her to sleep.

Chapter 3

When the paper butterfly awoke, the first golden rays of sunlight were just beginning to appear over the horizon. To her surprise, a majestic black and orange butterfly was also resting nearby.

"How did I miss this magnificent creature last night!" she exclaimed.

Transfixed by his feather-like markings illuminated in a shaft of morning light, the paper butterfly crept closer.

"What beautiful patterning!" she gasped.

She gazed at the worn orange sections of his wings and the bold shades of black that streaked down their tattered edges.

"It is as if they are painted canvases that tell his story," she sighed.

Although deeply curious, the paper butterfly thought it best not to disturb the sleeping monarch. She quietly crept above the leaf and opened up her wings to let the warmth of the sun's rays dry them.

All around her were glistening droplets, each one a perfect sphere shimmering in the morning sunlight.

"How magical!" she gasped.

She peered dreamily into one of these transparent pools. Staring back at her was her own reflection.

"Oh my goodness! What has happened to one of my wings!" she exclaimed. "When I was created it was so silky smooth, but now it is rippled like the water when the breeze blows. I wonder if my Maker would still think I was beautiful."

"He would indeed," she heard a distinguished voice say. "Yesterday's rain has given you life's first scar. Your wings may not be perfect anymore, but they will always be beautiful."

Sitting beside the paper butterfly was the majestic monarch. He had now emerged and was basking with outstretched wings in the warm morning sunlight.

"When I eclosed from my chrysalis, I was born with vivid orange wings that were as bright as the rising sun. I was so proud of how beautiful they were. It was as if the sun itself glowed within them."

The veteran monarch paused to look at his now-tattered wings.

"These wings have guided me through many struggles. Now each is etched with my story, and today I proudly wear the marks of imperfection as medals of honour that celebrate my life."

He pointed to a blemish.

"This V-shaped scratch was made by the beak of a bird that I escaped from when I was a newly fledged butterfly."

He scanned another wing. The paper butterfly edged closer.

"And this scar tells the tale of my escape from a spider."

"What about this one?" she asked, pointing to a large missing section at the edge of one of his hind wings.

"Ah, this is the tear from when I was tossed around by the wind in a storm."

The paper butterfly shuddered.

"My wings, like me, are old now and my life's journey is nearly at an end. Your wings, in contrast, have but one scar. Many more will appear before your life is over."

The paper butterfly had so many questions she wanted to ask, but before she had managed to gather her thoughts, the wise old monarch lifted himself into the sky and spiralled upwards.

He was joined by another.

The paper butterfly longed to follow, but something held her back.

At first, the two monarchs flew around quite randomly; then synchronizing their movements, they circled and spun around each other as if they were tied together by some invisible thread. Higher and higher they flew until their wings seemed to kiss the sun in appreciation of its warmth. Then tumbling and whirling through the sky, they flew in what the paper butterfly felt must be some spiritual dance to honour the heavens.

"How beautiful!" she exclaimed.

With eyes transfixed, she watched as the monarchs slowly drifted down from the sky, arm in arm, like feathers gently falling towards the earth. Then cradled upon the grass stems below her, they tenderly whispered secrets to each other.

The paper butterfly busied herself on a nearby flower as she felt she didn't want to intrude on such a personal moment.

After a while the two monarchs parted and the female flew over to a small patch of delicate pink blossoms that hung together like clusters of nodding bells. The monarch carefully selected a suitable leaf, testing each with her spindly legs to make sure it was worthy of her bounty. She placed a tiny, creamy white pearl carefully on its underside, hidden away from prying eyes.

It was as if the butterfly was leaving a final gift to the earth before she departed. Seconds later, in a flutter of wings, she was gone.

Chapter 4

The ovate pearl was cream-coloured, only about the size of a pinhead. The paper butterfly moved a little nearer to inspect this tiny gift more closely.

The egg looked so serenely beautiful and reminded her of the glowing moon at night.

"Maybe it is the Child of the Moon carried down by the butterfly from the heavens," she mused.

Interrupted from her thoughts by a strange tickly sensation on her back wings, the paper butterfly quickly spun around.

On the leaf behind her was a long furry creature with an explosion of colourful tufts of hair that looked like the bristles on a toothbrush. He had a small morsel of milkweed leaf hanging out of the corner of his mouth.

"Excuse me," implored the caterpillar, "I am in the middle of eating this leaf."

"You do seem to have quite a healthy appetite," chuckled the paper butterfly.

She looked in amazement at the huge hole in the leaf beside him.

"Is this the only plant you eat?" she inquired.

Eager to answer, the caterpillar quickly swallowed the remaining milkweed in his mouth.

"Yes, it is." He replied, "Milkweed gives us protection from predators because of its poisonous milky sap."

He pointed to the white substance oozing from the recently chewed leaf edge.

"Oh my!" exclaimed the paper butterfly. "My poor Child of the Moon pearl is on the leaf! Will it be poisoned by this milky stuff?"

The tussock moth caterpillar crawled closer to inspect the 'pearl' in more detail.

"Do not fear," he reassured. "This is a monarch egg. It will not be harmed by the poisonous sap. Milkweed is the monarch's host plant, too."

The paper butterfly was very much relieved.

"Thank you so much for explaining," she said politely.

"You are welcome," replied the caterpillar, "and now, if you will please excuse me, I am rather keen to continue my munching."

He eagerly clasped the edge of the leaf and, with a repetitive arcing motion, began his cycle of nibble and walk, walk and swallow, until he disappeared from view.

The paper butterfly excitedly settled down beside her beloved egg.

A day passed, and then another.

She edged a little nearer hoping to finally see some sign of life, but the egg remained motionless.

A group of reddish-orange insects with conspicuous black bands across their middles scuttled quickly behind her.

"You need to wait, you need to wait, you need to wait," they remarked as they scurried to and fro.

"I know," the paper butterfly sighed, "but, you see, this is a precious monarch egg, and I am so keen to make friends with my Child of the Moon butterfly when it emerges."

Four pairs of feet made their way over a nearby leaf. Crawling across carefully manufactured silken strands, the creature skillfully cast out her web like a fisherman of the air.

"All good things come to those who wait," the spider instructed as she finally settled into the top corner of her lair.

"I know," sighed the paper butterfly again.

So, to keep herself occupied, she began to study the other animals who also called this plant their home.

The milkweed was certainly a very busy place. Several reddish orange insects energetically fed on the young pink flower buffet. Another creature who looked as if it had four eyes, was also on a leaf nearby. The paper butterfly listened to the creature making a soft, almost continuous purring noise as it feasted on the milkweed.

"This must be good stuff," she thought as she examined the leaves more closely. "I wish I could sample it, too."

Suddenly she was alerted by a squeal of surprise. The little creature had fallen off its perch and had landed upside down on the leaf below. With all six legs flailing, it tried for several minutes to right itself. The paper butterfly flew down and ever so gently tipped the little creature back over with her wing. He purred in thankfulness and scuttled away.

The paper butterfly fluttered back up to her beloved egg.

"Good night my friend," she yawned sleepily.

Sensing the soothing breeze flowing over her wings and listening to the rhythmic chirping sounds that filled the air, she slowly drifted off to sleep.

Chapter 5

When she awoke, the sun was already high in the sky. The paper butterfly eagerly turned in the direction of the egg. Would today be the day the magnificent monarch made an appearance?

To her absolute horror, the egg was not there.

Annoyed with herself for oversleeping and missing the spectacle of the monarch emerging, she frantically searched around to find it; but it, too, was nowhere to be seen.

"That's very strange," she thought.

Nearby a tiny pale greyish-white coloured caterpillar with a black head was feasting happily in the middle of the milkweed leaf. Feeling a little sad over the loss of her egg, the paper butterfly distracted herself by watching the tiny creature's myriad of little legs moving it slowly along.

She edged closer.

Its skin was smooth and leathery.

Suddenly, the colour drained from her wings as a troubling thought entered her mind.

"Did you eat my egg?" she inquired.

"Me? No! I AM the egg," replied the tiny caterpillar, deeply confused. "Well, I used to be, so I guess I am not now, but I didn't eat the egg, well... only the outside of it."

This flow of consciousness did nothing to help relieve the paper butterfly's concerns. How could this creature be a monarch? It looked nothing like the beautiful veteran. It didn't even have the correct colouring!

"But you are not orange and black, and you most certainly don't have beautiful wings," she implored.

The caterpillar looked down at his small body and stubby little legs. He tried to turn over to see if any wings were hidden underneath that he hadn't yet discovered, but couldn't find any. So, after bowing his small black head in thought about how best he could explain, he began again.

"A few days ago, I was born and put inside an egg. I was ever so tiny, and the egg was such a cozy safe place for me to grow. I couldn't see out of it, but I could hear things happening and I knew you were out here waiting for me.

Someone kept telling us all good things come to those who wait, and so I waited patiently. By yesterday evening I had grown so much that I felt squished, so as soon as it got light this morning, I gnawed open the eggshell. It was SOOO tasty!

Anyhow, I wanted to crawl over to you to tell you I was hatched and to introduce myself, but you were still asleep; and, well, I just couldn't help myself. So while I was waiting for you, I ate the whole egg case because I was ravenous! I am sorry if I upset you by doing this."

"Oh, my poor little Child of the Moon,'" replied the paper butterfly in the most tender tone she could muster. "I am so embarrassed that I jumped to the wrong conclusion. You see, a very hairy caterpillar that I met when you were a tiny egg told me you were a monarch. So I thought a butterfly would emerge, not a caterpillar like you."

"Yeh! Me? A butterfly like you? Oh I wish!" replied the caterpillar.

Then, with the air cleared, he lowered his small black head, selected a particularly juicy section of the leaf beneath him, and began to eat voraciously once more.

Over the next two weeks, the paper butterfly often spent time with the caterpillar and enjoyed having a friend to share her life with. Some days he would eat for hours on end. At these times the paper butterfly would tell her companion stories about the beautiful world around them both. The caterpillar loved this as he had very poor eyesight and couldn't see much beyond the leaf he was chewing.

On other days the paper butterfly noticed that her friend did not seem to want to eat at all and would lie instead on a leaf, sluggish and grey looking, as if he felt unwell.

"I guess my Child of the Moon just overate yesterday and needs time to rest today," she thought.

So, to keep herself busy, the paper butterfly would fly up into the air and fill her mind with wonderful stories she could tell her friend when he felt better. She never strayed far though, as the caterpillar seemed much more nervous during these times without her nearby.

"Having you close by makes me feel safer when my skin gets too tight," he explained.

On mornings after these languid days, the paper butterfly was amazed at how much the caterpillar had grown. Secretly she worried that if her companion did not stop eating and growing he would get too big for the milkweed leaves to support him, and she was deeply troubled about what might happen then.

By the thirteenth day, the Child of the Moon was almost as large as the leaves themselves, and extremely hungry.

The paper butterfly hurriedly led her exeedingly ravenous friend to the closest juicy meal.

"Stay right here," she instructed. "While you are eating this delicious leaf, I am just going to stretch my wings in this beautiful morning light. I promise I won't be away too long."

Absent-mindedly the caterpillar nodded his head as he eagerly began devouring the edge of the leaf.

Content that her friend was safely occupied, the paper butterfly happily fluttered up into the warm morning sun to admire the sea of nodding flowers swaying in the breeze. The blues of the lupine a few weeks ago were now a mosaic of vibrant yellows and pinks. She swooped and arced through them, brushing her body against their cheerful heads and scattering their pollen across the landscape.

Stopping to catch her breath, she suddenly noticed how high the sun had risen in the sky.

"I had better get back," she thought. "That not-so-little caterpillar will probably have eaten almost all that leaf by now!"

She hurried back over the rippling meadow to where she had left her Child of the Moon earlier that morning and peered down.

"I am sure this was the place," she puzzled, as she scanned the stalk where the leaf had once hung.

The leaf was no more.

In front of her, a trail of destruction led from one stalk to the next.

"How could that greedy caterpillar possibly have eaten so much in such a short time?" the paper butterfly gasped.

Frantically she began checking the other milkweed plants nearby, desperately searching for her friend.

"Where has my Child of the Moon gone? I TOLD him to say right on that leaf and wait for me!" she exclaimed.

Picking her way carefully across the remnants of each piece of vegetation, the paper butterfly continued to search for the greedy caterpillar.

A familiar voice stopped her in her tracks.

"I'm here! Up here!"

"Help me! PLEASE!" it cried.

In a panic, the paper butterfly took to the sky and to her absolute horror spotted the Child of the Moon completely tangled up in the sticky spider's web!

Without a second thought for her safety, she flew headlong into the spider's snare. Beating her wings frantically against the menacingly strong threads, she sliced through the strands one by one until only a few tattered threads remained.

"You came to rescue me!" the Child of the Moon exclaimed gratefully. "But what if you get stuck?"

The paper butterfly wanted to reassure her friend that everything would be fine, but with each movement, she could feel the web's steely grip tightening.

A shiver ran through her fibres.

She turned.

Within striking distance, the huntress hovered upon her web of glistening silver, her fangs poised, ready to deliver their kiss of venom.

"All good things come to those who wait," she smirked.

Refusing to surrender, the paper butterfly hastily slashed through the remaining silken threads.

The final thread broke.

"Run! Run away!" she called as her friend fell to the ground below.

A sharp stabbing sensation pierced the tip of her back wing, and eight long, spindly legs enveloped her.

The paper butterfly froze.

Suddenly, the huntress recoiled.

"Agh!" the spider screamed in anger. "You are not tasty at all. Indeed, you are nothing more than disgusting paper!"

The huntress began to retreat, leaving the paper butterfly trapped in the tattered web.

"The web of life is a most mingled yarn," she muttered angrily, as she scuttled away.

"But if you are not going to eat me, please let me out of this trap," the paper butterfly pleaded.

"A trap is only a trap if you do not know about it," sneered the spider. "Since you do, consider it a challenge."

And with that, she left.

The paper butterfly hung limply in her prison of gossamer thread. Her wings were so heavy and sore from her frantic efforts to free the caterpillar that she had no energy or will left to attempt to free herself.

She closed her eyes and let the world continue around her.

Buzzing in unison, the sound of the many bees busily collecting pollen floated through the summery haze. Several birds joined the symphony of sound, singing a melody that almost seemed to mirror their undulating movements as they flew.

"Hey Sweetie, hey Sweetie, hey Sweetie," they happily called.

These familiar noises felt reassuring.

Suddenly, the paper butterfly became aware of another sound. Just above her, a caterpillar was busily munching.

She opened her eyes.

"I am so thankful to see you," she stammered. "I didn't think you would return."

"Our friendship is much stronger than any gossamer thread," the Child of the Moon replied. "I am just sorry I took such an age to do so, It's a long way up here for me to climb. I will have you free soon."

With a final munch, the trap was no more.

Suddenly, the paper butterfly felt herself falling, and the rush of air flowing past her helped to shake off the remaining silken threads.

"Thank you," she added gratefully.

"You are welcome," interjected the Child of the Moon. "Come on, let's find a place in the tree above us to rest this afternoon. I think we have both had enough excitement for one day."

Chapter 6

The following morning both the paper butterfly and the Child of the Moon woke up late.

"I don't feel like doing much today," the sleepy caterpillar announced. "I think I will just hang around for a while."

He slowly climbed just a leaf or two higher in the tree. Carefully spinning a small pad of silk on the underside of a twig, he attached himself to it and then hung upside down, motionless, in the shape of a J.

"I guess my Child of the Moon is just tired from his adventures yesterday," assumed the paper butterfly. "I must admit I am a little weary, too."

She flew up beside him and together they rested under the canopy of the tree, letting the events of the world around them continue for an entire day and a night.

As the sun peeked over the horizon the following day, the paper butterfly was roused from her slumber by a strange shaking sensation. Instinctively, she turned towards her friend.

Skin grey and shrivelled, antennae limply hanging beneath him, she watched in horror as the Child of the Moon writhed around.

"Oh, my dear child!" she exclaimed. "What is happening to you!"

Her horror transformed into amazement when he began to shed his skin, revealing an emerald-green silk tent with tiny golden flecks and a gilded crown.

"I am not sure what is happening, but I sense that it is something wonderful," she whispered tenderly. "Do not worry. I will wait here by your side for as long as you need."

The Child of the Moon stayed hidden in his strange retreat for many days. The paper butterfly waited patiently.

After about a week, she noticed the tent darkening, the faint outline of a wing, the orange, the black veins, the white polka dots.

"Well bless my soul!" she exclaimed, "My Child of the Moon IS a monarch after all!"

And she flew into the morning light to dance in the sky, hoping he would be watching the world outside his cocoon.

"I am here, I am waiting for you!" she cried gleefully, unable to hide her excitement any longer.

After about half an hour, the top portion of the transparent tent had expanded like an accordion.

"Are you trying to stretch out your beautiful wings?" the paper butterfly inquired as she finally settled beside him. "Your tent seems such a tight space for you to be. Can you not nibble your way out like you did from your pearl egg?"

It was as if the Child of the Moon heard her, for just at that moment, a small crack appeared along one side of his cocoon.

"That's it!" exclaimed the paper butterfly excitedly.

Pressing downwards and outwards, the monarch slowly began to force himself out. With each movement he made, a little more of his body appeared. Then, with one final tremendous thrust, he was free!

His spindly legs clung onto the now empty casing as he hung upside down to rest.

The paper butterfly was horrified.

"My dear child!" she exclaimed, "I just knew that tent was too small for you to truly develop properly! Look at those crumpled wings! How are you EVER going to fly with those!"

The Child of the Moon rocked himself to and fro in the warm sunlight. His swollen abdomen pulsed as he moved.

"I am not sure how, but your wings are inflating before my very eyes!" she exclaimed in amazement.

Within an hour, a majestic butterfly with silken wings held together like exquisite hands in prayer hung beside her.

"Your father was right. A newly eclosed monarch is, indeed, as bright as the rising sun!" she declared.

The Child of the Moon turned his head.

"I'm a butterfly, I really AM a butterfly!" he cried excitedly.

He attempted several small flaps to test his wings but felt a little reticent to do more.

"Do you think I can fly?" he asked nervously.

Remembering how terrified she had felt when a sudden gust of wind forced her into the air for the first time, the paper butterfly understood the Child of the Moon's concerns.

"If you don't test them out, you will never know," she replied encouragingly.

Motivated by her kind words the Child of the Moon flapped his wings again. Suddenly he found himself rising into the air.

"Look at me! I can fly! I can fly!" he exclaimed as he fluttered rather erratically around her.

With a twisting, turning, clapping motion, his newly formed wings painted swirling patterns of colour in the air as he flew.

"I knew you could do it," remarked the paper butterfly proudly.

Suddenly, a gust of wind caught the Child of the Moon off guard. He frantically tried to push upwards to avoid the branch below and landed with an unceremonious thud.

"Oh my!" he exclaimed. "You make flying look so easy. How do you manage changes in wind direction so well? Even the smallest of breezes caught me by surprise!"

"Don't worry," the paper butterfly encouraged. "I am sure you will soon be floating around with ease. Let's rest now. Then, when the air is calmer, we can fly together and I will help you."

"That would be wonderful!" exclaimed the monarch excitedly.

"Oh my! I can fly. I can really fly," he repeated as he rocked himself gently to sleep.

Chapter 7

When the paper butterfly opened her eyes the following morning, the Child of the Moon was already busily fluttering from flower to flower. As she watched him, she couldn't help but wonder if he would need or want her, now he was such a handsome butterfly.

She noticed him unfurl a long, straw-like structure from his mouth. The paper butterfly felt sad that her maker had not given her anything similar.

"How could my dear friend want to remain with me, a mere paper butterfly, when he realizes I am not complete?" she thought.

The Child of the Moon glided past.

"Come on, Sleepyhead," he called. "Some of these flowers have the most delicious nectar hidden in their depths."

He flew to a nearby clover.

"This nectar tastes divine."

He fluttered to a yellow flower with a dark black centre.

"See how the bright petals act as a sign to guide us to the sweet bounty."

He darted to another, more subtle, yellow flower.

"This one communicates to us in a much more 'secret' language. It used to look like a plain yellow flower when I was a caterpillar, but I can now see all the patterns and markings that only butterflies and bees can see! Isn't it just the most beautiful sight?"

The paper butterfly smiled and pretended that she could see the secret patterning.

All she saw was a simple yellow flower.

"Why did my maker create me to resemble a butterfly but not function like one?" she wondered.

Suddenly, a shadow appeared overhead, and a branch-like object loomed over them. With a SWISH, it grabbed the Child of the Moon in its net.

The paper butterfly felt a spasm of fear shudder through her body. She held her breath as a pair of hands reached into the net and gently picked up the Child of the Moon.

"I know those hands. It's my Maker'!" she suddenly exclaimed.

The paper butterfly watched as he carefully placed a tiny paper circle onto the middle of one of the butterfly's wings. Then, gently, he set the monarch back down on a leaf nearby.

Soon after, her Maker was gone.

The paper butterfly eagerly flew over to the Child of the Moon. He was already busily inspecting the shiny paper marking on his silky soft wing.

"Just look at what I have," he gasped.

He was unsure what the patterning on the tag signified but felt positive it was something extremely important.

"It is a gift from my Maker," the paper butterfly explained proudly.

"Really?" cried a delighted Child of the Moon. "Oh my!"

Unable to contain his excitement, he rose into the air and joyfully fluttered around his friend.

"My wish has come true. My wish has come true. Now, I am part paper butterfly too," he chanted gleefully.

The paper butterfly felt a wave of relief wash over her. It seemed clear that their paths in life were meant to follow one another.

"Yes, my dearest Child of the Moon," she exclaimed happily. "We truly are united now! Come on, let's fly in celebration of our friendship and I will show you the most wonderful meadow of glowing yellow flowers that rise to greet the sun. I know I can't drink their nectar like you, but I will see their beauty and I think you will enjoy their bounty."

The patch of goldenrod shone brightly in the morning sun. As the Child of the Moon sampled its delicious nectar, the paper butterfly dreamily watched the myriad of other insects also feasting on its blooms.

She noticed how the flowers swayed in appreciation as the pollinators flew from one bloom to another.

"You know, I believe you are as thankful for being pollinated as the pollinators are for your nectar," the paper butterfly mused.

Suddenly, she remembered the words of the Karner Blue.

"Of course!" she exclaimed. "The elements in our world are all connected. Each of us depends upon the actions and presence of others around us to survive and flourish."

At that moment, a gust of wind blew, and the densely crowded small heads of golden yellow flowers swayed in unison with the tall plumes of the grasses that supported them. It felt to the paper butterfly as if they were nodding in agreement with Karner Blue's words.

"You were so wise, my Karner friend," she whispered. "I promise to make my actions, however small, be ones that help others around me, for we truly are all connected."

Chapter 8

The weeks that followed were a time of such beauty and plentifulness, and the paper butterfly felt an increasing sense of peace settle upon her soul. Then, one morning, she noticed a change in the air.

It was colder than it had been for a long while. All around, orange and yellow leaves spun in circles like children's windmills. Then, when the wind changed direction, they seemed to chase each other, twisting and turning through the trees.

"It's the falling colours!" the paper butterfly exclaimed.

She glanced over to where her Child of the Moon was resting. He seemed to be slower to rise on this cool morning.

The leaves around her shone as bright as church glass in the hazy morning sun. The paper butterfly wondered if maybe they had shaken off their green coats and put on ones with more vivid colours to help them feel warmer.

"They are glowing as brightly as a newly hatched monarch's wings!" she exclaimed.

She knew the butterfly's bright colouring was a warning to others and wondered if the leaves had changed their colour as some special warning message, too.

Glancing down at the glowing red leaf beneath her, she curled her antennae around its edges to reassure it that its beauty had indeed been noticed. Suddenly, a gust of wind dislodged them both from the branch and they floated gently downwards, like feathers in the wind.

The paper butterfly couldn't contain her excitement.

"Look at me," she cried, "I am one of the falling colours tumbling from branches like confetti."

She watched as the red leaf, which she had caressed only moments before, landed softly on the damp ground below.

At that moment, a crowd of small children came noisily running along the woodland floor. They chattered excitedly as the leaves crunched and crackled beneath their feet.

With them was someone whose gentle, caring voice reminded the paper butterfly of her Maker.

"Come and sit here, my friends," he instructed.

He spoke softly as if not to disturb the stillness that had fallen once more upon this autumnal morning. Sensing his desire for calmness, the children settled in a cluster on some brightly coloured blankets he had carefully spread on the ground. The paper butterfly flew up into the safety of a branch just above him.

With all eyes now watching in eager expectation, he began.

"Only a few weeks ago, you might have caught a glimpse of a monarch butterfly in this clearing. In early fall, the monarchs gather to feed on the plentiful supply of nectar-rich plants that grow here. They need this energy in preparation for their long journey ahead."

The paper butterfly edged closer, keen to hear more.

"My Child of the Moon certainly has been getting plumper, but what is this journey he talks of?" she pondered.

"The weather is cooling," the man continued. "As a result, many monarch butterflies have already begun their migration south, for unlike you and me, butterflies rely on the sun's warmth to stay active and would be unable to survive during our long, cold winters."

The paper butterfly shuddered.

"Where do they go?" asked one small child.

"Yes, where do they go?" cried the paper butterfly with real urgency in her voice.

Noting the young children's interest, their teacher continued.

"They make the long journey south over four thousand kilometres to their over-wintering grounds in Mexico," he replied.

There was a gasp from the children who were listening.

"Four thousand kilometres? That is such a long way for such a small creature!" one of the children exclaimed.

"How do they know where to go?" another asked.

"That, indeed, is the question," answered their teacher. "The monarchs do not have anyone to show them the way yet something inside them knows where to go."

The paper butterfly had so many questions she wanted to ask this knowledgeable man, but although she wished to learn more, she also wanted to inform the Child of the Moon about what she had already heard.

She hurried back up to the upper part of the tree where he was still resting.

"I have so much to tell you," she began.

"I was one of the falling colours tumbling down like confetti onto the forest floor. I saw a group of children who chattered excitedly as the leaves crunched and crackled beneath their feet. With them was someone like my Maker. He explained how monarch butterflies who break out of their cocoons late in the summer, like you, make a journey over four thousand kilometres to a mountainous forest in central Mexico!"

She paused, expecting a reaction to this news.

There was none.

She moved a little closer, thinking that maybe the Child of the Moon simply hadn't heard her.

"You see," she continued, "when the days become shorter and the leaves begin to glow as brightly as a newly hatched monarch's wings, you need to travel from your summer breeding grounds to central Mexico because it is just too cold to stay here in the winter.

I know how much you love the flowers here, but the once vibrant petals that gave you their gift of delicious nectar are now becoming but silvery ghosts of their former selves. They have moved on from feeding you. See how they now feed the songbirds who flit from stem to stem as they feast from their seed heads."

Surprisingly, the Child of the Moon still didn't stir.

A sudden realization dawned upon the paper butterfly.

"Oh, my dearest friend, are you too cold to move?" she gasped.

Instinctively, she partially unfolded one of her wings and wrapped it tenderly around her friend to warm him. As he began to stir, she carefully helped him to move into the sun.

"Thank you," he said weakly. "The last few nights have cloaked my wings with such an icy breath that it has been hard to keep going. I knew, deep inside, that I needed to fly south, but I didn't want to leave you."

"Then we must go together!" exclaimed the paper butterfly. "I know I do not feel the cold like you, but the ice and snow that coats this world in winter would not be good for my paper wings, either."

She looked tenderly at her friend.

"I know of a beautiful patch of yellow blooms that have not yet gone to seed," she stated. "Their sweet nectar would warm your soul and give you much-needed energy. Do you feel able to take a short flight to them?"

"Yes, I think I could fly now," replied the Child of the Moon with a little more life in his voice.

The paper butterfly guided her companion to the swathe of late-blooming goldenrod, then fluttered into the crisp morning air to take one last look at the place she had come to think of as home.

Below her, the densely crowded small heads of yellow flowers swayed rhythmically in the gentle breeze. The paper butterfly watched the Child of the Moon happily fluttering from flower to flower, feasting on its sweet bounty.

"I am so grateful that you were willing to share your beauty and nectar with us today," she remarked.

The golden-yellow blooms nodded their heads in appreciation of her thanks.

The trees, dressed in their carnival clothes, suddenly rustled in the breeze as if to bid her goodbye.

“Thank you for giving us shelter," the paper butterfly called.

The leaves fell silent, content that their message had been conveyed.

At that moment, two small milkweed seeds floated peacefully past her on their homemade parachutes. As one gently brushed against her wings, she felt its softness caress her.

"Thank you for giving my Child of the Moon the gift of life," the paper butterfly whispered tenderly.

"And thank YOU for being such a caring friend," interjected the Child of the Moon as he fluttered excitedly around her.

"Shall we go?"

With an energetic clap of his wings, he soared above her.

Their journey had begun.

Migration

Chapter 9

At first they stayed low to the ground, but as the arc of the sun rose, the paper butterfly suddenly felt some magic force lifting her higher.

"What is happening?" she cried excitedly. "The air feels as if it is bubbling up all around me."

"I am not sure," the Child of the Moon called rather distractedly from below. "I felt it briefly, too, but the air is like a roller coaster. One second, I am rising, and the next, I am plummeting back down."

At that very moment another wave of warm air caught his wings. The bubbling currents buffeted him sideways and then shot him skywards rather like an elevator going up at speed.

"Oh my!!!" he wailed.

The paper butterfly peered up at the almost cloudless sky to see what could be causing this strange occurrence. High above, a pair of hawks were circling as if on invisible strings.

"Kee-eeeee-arr, kee-eeeee-arr," they called.

The paper butterfly gave a shrill cry of pure excitement.

Suddenly, she felt another powerful surge beneath her wings. She was more prepared this time and tried hard to mirror the hawk's spiralling pattern, wondering if this was the key to riding these vertical waves.

"This is magical," she cried, unable to hide her delight.

She was nearer to the hawks now and marvelled at how smooth and well-balanced their flight was, even in this turbulent air.

"You are so good at this," she declared as she finally drew level with them. "Do you know what this strange phenomenon is?"

"They are rising pockets of air warmed by the sun's rays," one of the hawks replied.

He peered curiously at the paper butterfly from across his long, broad wing.

At that moment, the Child of the Moon shot up once more from below. The paper butterfly noticed how unsteady his wings were compared to the hawks'.

"How do we stay in these rising pockets?" he asked with an equally unsteady voice.

"When you locate a thermal, try spiralling. This helps to keep you inside the rising bubble of air," replied the other hawk. "Follow us and we will show you."

The Child of the Moon and the paper butterfly shadowed the hawks' movements. When the next thermal came, they rose as one, each syncing their movements in time with the bubbling air.

As they continued to climb, puffy clouds magically began forming above them.

"The air is so pure up here," sighed the paper butterfly happily.

Far beneath her, a mosaic of fiery hues nestled against a patchwork quilt of golden brown and green that looked like some skillfully crafted woven tapestry. A meandering river curled through the landscape, glistening in the sunlight. In this miniature world, roads spun out from villages like gossamer threads ready to ensnare unsuspecting prey.

The paper butterfly turned to thank the hawks for sharing the beauty of the skies with her, but they were now far in front, mere dots on the distant horizon.

"Goodbye, my friends," she called.

Suddenly, she became aware of an excited flutter beside her.

"Look how those soft fluffy clouds ahead of us are lining up in a row!" exclaimed a delighted Child of the Moon. "It is as if they are forming a pathway showing us the way."

They followed the hawks' lead, and after a short while, the paper butterfly managed to manoeuvre herself directly underneath the first of the clouds.

"And now?" she inquired, hoping the Child of the Moon was close behind her.

"Fly straight and fast," he called gleefully as he shot past her. "I think I am finally learning the art of this."

The paper butterfly positioned her wings as flat as she could and immediately found herself zooming through the air like a torpedo speeding from cloud to cloud.

"This is such fun!" she cried as the air whistled past her antennae. "Let's race to Mexico!"

On the horizon, they spotted a small glint of blue-green glistening in the afternoon light. As they moved closer, the thin ribbon of sparkling water morphed into a vast aqua sheen that carpeted almost half the landscape. Wind-dancing waves rushed across its surface and then pummeled the land along its edge with all their might. It was as if Life herself had entered the water, for the crashing waves were as rhythmical as any beating heart.

"What is it?" queried the Child of the Moon.

"I am not sure," replied the paper butterfly. "It looks and behaves like the water on the pond where the geese fly, but it stretches on for an eternity with no sign of land on the other side."

"Well, we simply have to find a way to cross it!" exclaimed the Child of the Moon earnestly.

They drifted down from the clouds and headed towards the shoreline. The sun, no longer above them, was also settling down for the evening.

Arriving at a peninsula that tapered out into a long sharp point, they landed nervously onto a rock at the water's edge.

"The water stretches as far as my eyes can see," uttered the Child of the Moon nervously.

"How can we possibly cross all that way?" the paper butterfly added in dismay.

"You can't today," she heard a voice call. "The sun is already too low in the sky to contemplate such a long journey."

Hanging in the tree above them were hundreds of monarchs.

For the most part, they were perfectly silent and almost completely still. It was as if they had become part of the tree itself. Then, as the paper butterfly saw yet another monarch approach, the large curtain above her flashed their wings in unison to greet the new arrival. She was enchanted.

"Please come and join us," the new arrival suggested. "I feel a chill in the air again this evening and our roost will provide not only safety in numbers, but also some protection from the cold. Hopefully by tomorrow morning the winds will be blowing in a more favourable direction. Then, and only then, will we be able to make it to the other side safely."

"Thank you," the Child of the Moon replied as he climbed gratefully up to join them.

Slowly, the sun settled herself below the horizon, painting the sky in a million shades as she bid the monarchs goodnight. Then, as twilight crept his way stealthily across the sky, he seemed to say,

"Time to close your eyes and rest, for tomorrow will be a long and busy day."

Chapter 10

The following morning, the paper butterfly awoke with a feeling of trepidation. Looking out over the vast wilderness of water she sensed real danger. Her thin paper wings shuddered at the thought of all that moisture. If only she could be sure there was land on the other side.

The resting monarchs, who seemed to adorn every inch of the branches around her, began to stir. Each positioned themselves facing the sun, to soak in the warmth of its rays.

Then, all at once, they began to take flight, swooping and whirling overhead, a swirling kaleidoscope of motion. Some flew back inland, trying to find lift. Others deliberately headed out over the blue-green waves, flapping their wings to gain height. It was each butterfly for itself, a personal battle with the elements.

"Who do we follow?" asked the paper butterfly nervously.

It was as if nature answered, for a sudden gust of wind seized the Child of the Moon and propelled him out over the water. He tried in vain to turn back, but the wind was too strong.

In a moment of panic, the paper butterfly launched into the air and headed out over the water in pursuit of her friend.

In front of her, the Child of the Moon fought desperately to gain control. He was dangerously close to the water. Waves broke violently only a few feet below. He tried to gain height, but the buffeting wind was too strong.

He looked down at the swirling water and watched, mesmerized. Was it mirroring the chaos of his own thoughts?

Suddenly, he heard a familiar voice.

"You can do this," the paper butterfly yelled, "I am right behind you. Be strong and stay with me!"

With renewed vigour, the Child of the Moon frantically flapped his wings. The paper butterfly followed, determination flowing through her body, driving her forward and closer to her companion.

He was flying higher now, his wings undulating more rhythmically and his body contracting with each beat, pushing air underneath him and propelling him forward.

"I knew you could do it," cried the paper butterfly, relieved that her friend seemed in control once more.

Below, the wind danced and twirled across the water's surface. Strange glistening creatures painted in neon colours hurried across its waves, the one in front guiding the way and the other racing behind.

"Those speeding creatures with long, frothy white tails move in formation like the long necks when they fly," the paper butterfly remarked.

She was flying beside her beloved Child of the Moon by now. He, too, had noticed the zooming creatures.

"I wonder if they are talking to each other for support as they migrate," he pondered. "I know geese honk to encourage those leading to keep up their speed. Maybe these noisy neon creatures are trying to motivate each other as they journey too."

"They must be," the paper butterfly agreed. "Maybe they are also leaving those water trails as signs to show us the way. Come on, let's follow them!"

She surged ahead, desperately trying to keep up with the noisy, rainbow-coloured creatures. But soon, the jet skis were mere dots on the horizon. Then they were gone.

All around them was nothing but water. Its rippling surface glistened in the early afternoon sun.

"How can we possibly know which way to go?" the paper butterfly implored. " Every direction looks the same."

"Do not fret," answered the Child of the Moon. "Something deep inside me knows the way. Let's fly in formation as the long necks do, and I will lead you."

Using his internal compass, the Child of the Moon took the lead. The paper butterfly followed closely behind.

"It is as if you are pulling me along by some invisible force!" she cried excitedly. "Now I understand why the long necks fly like this."

They travelled together for many hours until the sky was ablaze with the fire of the setting sun. At last they saw the shoreline, but although in sight, to an exhausted Child of the Moon it felt impossibly out of reach.

"Let me take the lead," said the paper butterfly tenderly. "Fly behind me as I have been doing and my wings can lift yours for a change."

Gratefully the Child of the Moon fell back, but even with less wind resistance, he felt as if his wings could not carry him much further.

"If only I had been able to drink some nectar before I left this morning. If only the wind hadn't taken me," he sighed.

Below them, a wooden vessel bobbed along on the water. It was the colour of the earth. From its deck, two tall trunk-like masts rose towards them. Its branches were adorned with sails that were the colour of the fall leaves.

"Look over there," the paper butterfly indicated. "I can see a bobbing island that we could rest on."

The paper butterfly was very thankful for this land amid the water. She was even more grateful to see her Child of the Moon now resting peacefully.

Billowing sails rippled in unison with the water below, rocking the boat comfortingly as it moved toward the shore. An old fisherman sat on the deck, happily singing to himself, as he gutted his catch of fish. The paper butterfly noticed how the wrinkles on his hands almost seemed to mirror the undulations of the waves around them.

Gulls wheeled in arcs overhead. Then, greedily, one swooped down in an attempt to steal a fish.

The fisherman waved his hands, shooing him away.

"Begone!" he cried with a chuckle in his voice. "You need to wait your turn."

From the tone in his voice, the paper butterfly could sense that he meant no harm. She watched as he generously threw a small piece from one of the fish back into the water beside the boat.

The gulls swooped in frenzied dives as they battled to win the prize.

"They are hungry," thought the paper butterfly. "I hope we reach land soon so that my Child of the Moon will also be able to feed."

Thankfully, it wasn't long before they reached the shore. An old rickety dock jutted out into the water to greet them. Tall spikes of brilliant red, trumpet-shaped flowers waved from the water's edge, and purple asters danced in joy alongside them. It was such a colourful welcome.

The fisherman gently steered the boat alongside the dock and then reached for one of the ropes to moor it.

"And what do we have here!" he exclaimed as he spotted the sleeping monarch. "Did you hitch a ride across the lake with me?"

He gently scooped the Child of the Moon into his weather-worn hands. The monarch stirred, opened his wings to the sun, and began tasting the air with his antennae.

"Well, bless your little heart," the fisherman whispered affectionately. "I think I just might know what you are searching for."

With a sense of purpose in his stride, he quickly carried the Child of the Moon to a group of cardinal flowers growing along the shoreline.

"Is this what you are hoping for?" he inquired as he tenderly placed the monarch onto their red, silky-soft petals.

The Child of the Moon immediately unfurled his proboscis. The old man chuckled, turned, and headed back to his boat.

The paper butterfly flew closer.

"I know we cannot stay for long," she remarked, "but the fisherman who carried you here seems kind, and his hands remind me so much of my Maker's. I think this would be a good place for us to rest tonight."

At that moment, a few other monarchs fluttered down to join them. It was as if they agreed that this was, indeed, an acceptable place to rest. The paper butterfly glanced across the water expecting to see others, but the skies were empty.

She turned back towards her Child of the Moon. He seemed so content, fluttering from flower to flower, feeding on the delicious nectar. She was thankful that he seemed to have energy again, but also worried about the journey ahead.

"How many more dangers will we face?" she thought.

This question weighed heavily on her mind, and it was a long time before she finally fell asleep that night.

Chapter 11

When she awoke, the sun was already high in the sky. The paper butterfly sleepily glanced around, expecting to see the monarchs who had roosted with them the night before, but only the Child of the Moon remained. He was happily fluttering from flower to flower, and had completely lost all sense of time.

"Where is everyone?" the paper butterfly inquired.

"Oh, they left a few hours ago," the Child of the Moon replied rather distractedly.

The paper butterfly looked exasperated.

"Did you not notice how high the sun has risen and think to wake me? We must leave immediately!" she exclaimed.

They continued south through skies that were as blue as early summer irises. Below them, a tapestry of colour scrolled past. Patchwork quilts of golden satin fields rippled in the breeze like gently lapping waves, and jewel-like sparkling streams curved through forests of burnt red.

Minutes became hours, and hours became days as puffy sailboat clouds raced along with them. These were happy and stress-free days for the friends, and the paper butterfly soon forgot that she had been so worried.

On the fifth day, the relatively flat land metamorphosed into a long line of rounded peaks that seemed to rise up to greet them.

"It is as if the earth is reaching up to welcome us and guide us on our way," remarked the paper butterfly excitedly.

Eager to explore this new terrain they hurriedly flew towards the crest of the nearest ridge. Suddenly they felt a rush of air flowing over their wings. The current was strong and carried them almost effortlessly along the crest of the ridge.

"I think we will journey far today," declared the Child of the Moon.

"I agree," added the paper butterfly. "The trees below us are simply flying past."

How many miles they soared, they were not sure. But as the sun finally headed towards the horizon, the ridge flattened.

In front of them was a high plateau carpeted with blooms.

"Oh, my dearest Child of the Moon," cried the paper butterfly ecstatically. "Just look at all that beautiful nectar waiting for you to feast on this evening. These mountains certainly did show us the way!"

The Child of the Moon was thankful for the ridge that had led them to this beautiful place and for the delicious nectar that lay within each bloom. As he fluttered joyfully from flower to flower, the paper butterfly sat quietly on a branch to take in the beautiful landscape around her.

The blooms meandered like a flowing river across the plateau, rippling softly in the gentle evening breeze. On one side of the meadow, dense growths of evergreen forest stood guard as if to protect this beautiful land. Under their canopy, ferns, mosses, and fungi tucked themselves into shady corners as if they were too nervous to openly share their intricate beauty.

On the other side of the meadow, a strange ghost forest of dead trees hugged the horizon.

"I wonder what happened to those?" The paper butterfly pondered. "The branches look so crestfallen without their needles."

At that moment, she heard a rustle on the ground below her. Glancing down, she spotted a small yellow and brown striped snail gliding slowly along the ground. As he inched along, his tentacles waved in synchrony as though they were swaying in time to some gentle melody.

Eager to make his acquaintance, the paper butterfly hurriedly flew down to join the small creature.

"I am very pleased to meet you!" she greeted enthusiastically.

Startled, the snail immediately hid itself in its shell.

"Oh my!" chuckled the paper butterfly, "I guess my eagerness must have frightened it."

She patiently settled herself on top of a nearby log until the snail had become used to her presence.

After a few minutes, he cautiously poked out first one tentacle, and then another.

"I am sorry if I alarmed you," the paper butterfly continued in the calmest voice she could muster.

The small brown and yellow snail slowly raised its head and turned to face the paper butterfly.

"You live in a beautiful place," the paper butterfly added.

"Why, thank you," he finally replied. "I have overheard several scientists who travel here to study the rare species that live in this wilderness say this, too."

The paper butterfly had so many questions that she wanted to ask. What rare species did it know? Are scientists people like her Maker? What was it like to live on a mountain like this? But she was acutely aware that even one query might take this creature a while to answer, so she settled on just one question.

"Do you know why some of the evergreen trees have died? They look so crestfallen without their needles."

After a great deal of consideration, the snail replied.

"Water is life-giving, but sometimes when the rain falls or the mists form, it takes life away."

Then, clearly content that the question had been answered, he withdrew once more into the safety of his shell.

The paper butterfly looked again at the lifeless trees. Their ashen pale branches seemed to hang so forlornly.

Why had the very thing that should have given them life, so cruelly taken it away?

Was every living thing's interaction with the world simply determined by chance?

As she pondered these questions, the last remnants of daylight faded, and the clouds lifted revealing a smooth, velveteen sky. Under this comforting blanket of darkness, the paper butterfly watched the moon slowly rise towards the heavens.

Above her, the Child of the Moon now hung peacefully, blissfully unaware of her concerns.

"Keep watch over your child tonight, dear Mother Moon," she whispered as she closed her eyes.

Chapter 12

When she awoke, the sun's golden petals had already bloomed in the sky. Beside her, the Child of the Moon sat with open wings absorbing their warming rays.

"What a beautiful morning!" he exclaimed. "Let's fly!"

But before he could move, hundreds of birds lifted themselves into the air.

"Time to go, time to go!" they trilled in agreement.

They flew as one, twisting, turning, swooping, and swirling, creating beautiful shape-shifting living clouds. One moment, they were a perfectly round sphere as dark as the night sky. Then, in a whirlpool of wings, they transformed into a running river meandering across the air above them until they were just a mere speck on the horizon.

Alive with their energy, the paper butterfly lifted herself into the air and danced across the sky, joyfully mirroring their movements.

"Look at me," she cried as she swooped and swirled through the air. "Have I ever told you how your mother and father danced in the sky like this?"

"No! Do tell me about them," pleaded the Child of the Moon.

"Well," the paper butterfly began, "at first, they flew around quite randomly."

And she darted this way and that like a leaf blown by the wind until the Child of the Moon felt quite dizzy.

"And then?" he laughed.

"They spun around each other as if they were tied together by some invisibe thread."

And she whirled around him as tightly as she could.

"Come on. Let's dance in the sky as they did!" she called.

They spiralled upwards, higher, and higher into the air until they were so far up in the sky that their wings seemed to almost kiss the sun in appreciation of its warmth.

Above them, the atmosphere was as clear as a deep blue sapphire. Here, they danced like the waves as they moved across open water. Then, laughing, they both began tumbling and whirling back downwards in perfect synchrony.

Beneath them, a white fluffy blanket covered the valley floor. They flew nearer, expecting to find a soft landing place where they could rest, but no place of safety appeared. Instead, a sea of ghostly greyness greedily engulfed them in its dampness.

A sudden sense of realization ran through the paper butterfly's fibres like the chill of an icy wind. The white blanket they had seen from the air was not land but the top of a thick layer of cloud that had silently formed below them.

"Stay close," she cried, praying with all her might that this wasn't the killing mist that the snail had mentioned.

They continued to fly through what felt like everlasting nothingness.

"It feels so damp," the Child of the Moon remarked.

The air swirled and eddied around them, making it harder and harder for them to know which way they were heading.

"I do not like this," the Child of the Moon whispered.

Suddenly, a tall pillar of glass and steel loomed up through the greyness.

"Watch out!" the paper butterfly screamed.

The sheer surface missed the monarch by mere inches as it rushed past.

The car lights below fanned out like a bright spider-web, with crawling streams of red and white specks along its gossamer threads. People littered the streets and sidewalks, hurrying along like bustling ants. Vans rudely honked as they got in each other's way. Everyone and everything seemed to be in a constant state of motion.

With powerful passion, the wind channelled them between the tall skyscrapers. Its giddy currents tossed them haphazardly like insignificant particles of dust.

"Look out!" screamed the paper butterfly again, as they were thrown directly in front of a stream of roaring traffic.

She ducked as a discarded piece of litter recklessly rushed between them.

Trembling like aspen leaves, they were tossed around and flung perilously close to another wall of steel.

An unsettling feeling began to well up inside the paper butterfly, for in this strange alien land, there were no trees, no places of safety, and no visible vegetation to find shelter or food. Instead, tall branchless metal poles lined the roads, hard concrete covered the soft, bare earth, and glass facades played tricks on her eyes and mind.

With flight muscles working overtime and heads bowed, they turned another corner.

The wind met them like a wall.

"It is too strong!" cried the Child of the Moon.

Exhausted, he turned and was immediately swept away.

Twisting,

Turning,

Spinning,

Falling.

A tall brick building across the street loomed closer.

Too close.

She heard a panicked cry and turned to see the Child of the Moon's tiny body smack against cold steel bars.

He tumbled lifelessly onto the floor.

In desperation, the paper butterfly tried to steer her way towards him, but the angry wind pulled her away.

"No!" she bellowed. "You will not take me away from my friend."

She grabbed onto the next metal railing within her grasp and pulled herself to safety.

The wooden floor of the balcony almost seemed to grow out of the walls of the building. Scattered over the ground, stacks of old terracotta pots were strewn haphazardly like leaves piled up on the forest floor. Some were filled to their brims with woven dreams of golds, reds, and the softest creams. Others contained only tired worn foliage, a mere memory of what once was.

The paper butterfly looked down at the lifeless Child of the Moon lying at the base of one of these pots. An overwhelming feeling of sadness filled her fibres. Her tiny body trembled in grief. It had all happened so fast.

"Grammy!" she heard a voice call. "Grammy, come quickly!"

The paper butterfly looked down. A small child was kneeling beside the Child of the Moon.

"What are you hollering about?" his grandmother inquired.

The young child pointed.

"Is it dead?" he asked.

Grammy calmly walked over and scooped up the limp monarch. Sensing the warmth of her hand, the Child of the Moon stirred.

"Bless his little heart," she replied. "He is just stunned. I am guessing the wind blowing around these buildings caught the little fella off guard."

She settled herself on an old wooden rocking chair. The small boy moved closer.

"Will he still be able to fly with such a torn wing?" he asked apprehensively.

Grammy smiled.

"Yes, I think so," she replied. "Monarchs are resilient little critters."

She gently placed the Child of the Moon onto the palm of her grandchild's hand.

"You know," she continued, "this handsome fella has probably flown well over eight hundred miles to reach our balcony and, on such a long journey, will inevitably receive some damage to his wings."

"That's a LONG way for such a tiny creature to fly!" gasped the small boy. "It must be such an adventure, though."

"Oh, the stories I could tell you," murmured the paper butterfly, much relieved that the Child of the Moon seemed to be recovering.

The small boy gently placed the monarch on a freshly cut flower in his small mesh butterfly habitat case, sharpened his pencil and recorded in large, unsteady letters the Child of the Moon's tag number APBL 101 in his notebook.

"Sleep tight, little one," he said affectionately to the now resting monarch. "Grammy says you will be feeling much better by the morning."

Then, with his notebook in hand, he quietly followed his grandmother indoors.

The paper butterfly fluttered over to the carry case.

"I am here," she whispered. "You are safe now."

Chapter 13

"Are you ready to go?" Grammy called. "It's getting light, and we will be leaving soon to tag the butterflies."

"Coming," replied the young boy.

He reached over to grab the carry case and spotted the paper butterfly on the floor below it. There was a warmth in his eyes, a sparkle too. His broad grin ignited her heart. The young boy quietly lifted her into his hands and placed her in the enclosure next to the Child of the Moon.

It didn't take them long to reach the park.

"Make sure you find a nice sunny bush to rest the butterfly on," instructed Grammy as they walked through the park entrance. "He won't be able to fly until his wings are warmed."

"Okay," replied the young child.

He stopped beside an empty wooden bench. A sweet, honey-like fragrance filled the air, and deep pink lace-capped blooms shone brightly in the morning light.

"What a beautiful place!" exclaimed the paper butterfly.

The young child's small hand reached into the enclosure.

"This is the young boy who helped us when you were thrown onto the balcony yesterday. Let him help you one more time," coaxed the paper butterfly gently.

Sensing the sun's warmth, the monarch climbed onto the child's hand and let the young boy carry him over to the fragrant bush. Feeling the soft petals beneath his feet, the Child of the Moon immediately turned to face the sun, basking in its warmth.

"Look, Grammy!" cried the boy excitedly.

The Grandmother chuckled.

"He is a wise old monarch and is sunning his wings to warm his flight muscles. I imagine that by the time we have finished tagging, he will be toasty enough to fly around with the others."

The Grandmother moved slowly, peering into bushes. In her hands she carried a long, flowing cone of white mesh hanging from a pole. The boy followed, notebook and pencil in hand. The paper butterfly happily fluttered into the tree above them.

A flash of orange. A flutter of wings. The swoosh of the net.

"They have caught one!" squealed the paper butterfly in delight.

She watched the young boy retrieve a monarch from his grandmother's net. He placed a tiny paper circle onto the middle of one of the butterfly's wings and then strolled back towards the Child of the Moon, carefully cradling his prize.

"Here’s a lady friend for you!" he said with a smile. "Let me introduce you to ACSC 902".

Then, feeling that the introductions were complete, he left them to get to know each other.

"I am so pleased to meet you," declared the Child of the Moon. "Have you travelled far?"

"From the northernmost tip of the Appalachian mountain range," replied the newly tagged monarch.

She fluttered onto a nearby leaf to soak up the sun's warming rays. In the glowing morning light, her feather-like wings shone as brightly as a stained-glass window.

The paper butterfly gasped.

"It is as if this creature has been sent to my Child of the Moon as a gift from the sun itself!" she exclaimed.

The newly tagged monarch turned to inspect the small paper circle.

"It seems you now have a tag, too," observed the Child of the Moon.

"It felt like such a momentous day when I received mine," he continued. "When I was young, I befriended the most kind-hearted paper butterfly. I admired her beautiful paper wings and wished with all my heart that I had some, too.

One day after I eclosed, her Maker caught me in a net similar to the one the lady caught you in. When he placed this paper tag on my wing, it felt like he had given me a small part of the paper butterfly, and we would be connected forever. Now you have been given part of her, too!"

A tear of happiness trickled down the paper butterfly's fibres. She had never really appreciated how much he admired her.

"Welcome to our family, O Daughter of the Sun!" she exclaimed as she joyfully flew down to join them.

The newly tagged monarch was thrilled.

"How lovely to meet you, dear Paper Butterfly," she cried.

Then, with a fresh appreciation of her tag's value, the Daughter of the Sun inspected it once again.

"Is Daughter of the Sun the name I have been given on this circle?" she inquired.

"I don't think so," the paper butterfly replied, "but when your iridescent wings glint in the sunlight they shine so brightly that you must be a gift from the sun herself."

"A gift, indeed!" exclaimed the Child of the Moon, who was rather taken with this new arrival.

"And what does the paper butterfly call you?" the Daughter of the Sun asked.

"The Child of the Moon," he replied rather sheepishly.

"I remember the day I named him as if it were only yesterday," added the paper butterfly.

"He was a tiny, creamy, white pearl and looked so serenely beautiful. His egg was like a miniature moon glowing softly in the evening light. Of course, I was young and innocent then, and naively presumed that he was the Moon's child carried down by a monarch from the heavens."

The Daughter of the Sun sighed.

"That is indeed a beautiful story. I feel blessed to know you, dear Child of the Moon."

All three then lifted themselves skywards in celebration of their friendship.

Chapter 14

Tracking the position of the sun with their antennae, the two monarchs took turns leading the way. They travelled across rolling hills and followed pristine streams that seemed to hurry along ever-widening valley floors.

On the third morning the terrain flattened, and the warm air became sultry with summer-like moisture. A wide river meandered haphazardly across the landscape as if it couldn't quite decide on the direction it wanted to take. Silvery sandbars adorned its edges, and neatly ordered rows of cherry red barges moved sleepily along.

To the left, the river flowed into a broad lagoon. At its entrance, an old moss-draped cypress tree rose from the water, standing guard over the scene like some stately ancient sentinel.

"How I would love to rest on your beautiful branches," the paper butterfly sighed as she flew towards it.

But the Child of the Moon and Daughter of the Sun flew on. The paper butterfly followed.

The river curved to the southwest. In the shallows, a pair of dabbling ducks were bobbing along with their heads underwater. The paper butterfly would have loved to ask them about what lived in the liquid world below, but the Child of the Moon and Daughter of the Sun were already pressing onwards.

The river meandered to the right. Where had this water come from, and where was it going? Was each droplet within it driven to migrate by some internal navigation system like the Child of the Moon and the Daughter of the Sun, or were they just flowing along, like her, into the unknown? These were the questions the paper butterfly pondered over as she followed her friends.

The river widened. The monarchs turned away from the water and flew west. The paper butterfly wearily followed.

They kept flying until the hazy sky was aglow with amber hues.

"We need to find nectar before it gets dark," uttered the Child of the Moon wearily. "I have been looking for hours now, but since we left the river, I have seen nothing but barren land."

"It is as if some enormous beast has selfishly taken everything and left nothing for anyone else," stated the Daughter of the Sun indignantly.

"Such thoughtlessness," agreed the Child of the Moon. "Surely the bounty should be there for all to share, not just for one to take all."

With heavy hearts, they continued wearily on.

"Please, point us in the direction of just one field still covered in blooms," the paper butterfly prayed as she quietly followed her tired friends.

As if in answer to her plea, a shaft of sunlight suddenly broke through the haze and illuminated a single area still clothed in clouds of cotton. Along its edges, electric purple blossoms reached skywards, basking in the warm evening light.

Drawn by their sugary scent, the Child of the Moon and Daughter of the Sun floated gratefully down. The paper butterfly followed. Then, as dusk cast his shadow on the earth, the three friends sheltered underneath the canopy of petals.

"Thank you, dear Sun", the paper butterfly whispered gratefully.

Chapter 15

The paper butterfly awoke early the following morning. All around was a quiet, restful silence. The deep blue shadows of the night still lingered, but the flush of gathering light on the eastern horizon somehow made it feel exciting.

She eagerly turned to face the rising sun and waited. Almost immediately, the cotton bolls around her began to change their hue. They magically morphed from the coolest of blues to the mellowest of cotton candy pinks. Then, as the sun spread her golden petals across the sky, each absorbed the light and turned the purest white, haloed with glowing yellow.

Inquisitively, she fluttered over to one of the nearby plants. Its now pure white bolls were as soft as down. She caressed the cloud-like surface. It felt like a hug, a safe place to dream.

Suddenly, she became aware of a distant hum.

The sound got closer: droning, whirring, clanking, groaning.

Grinding its way along the dusty earth was a creature, unlike anything the paper butterfly had ever seen. Her soul begged for her to flee from its grasp. Her body remained frozen in fear.

Within seconds, a gargantuan metal monster with large rolling feet loomed over her, Its large yellow teeth grinding across the ground, eating everything in its reach. The paper butterfly felt herself being sucked into the depths of its rumbling belly. Churning and growling, it smeared its oily juices across her wings as dust, broken stems, seeds, and cotton fibres flew through the air.

Then, like an unwanted piece of garbage, she was spewed onto the ground. All around her, mangled stalks and broken petals lay discarded on the bare earth.

Frantically, she picked herself up and headed back to the edge of the field.

"We need to leave right now!" she cried to her beloved friends.

With eyes fixed on the horizon and heart pounding, she led the monarchs away at great speed. She guided them through endless jewel-blue skies, not daring to look beneath her in fear that the churning, growling creature might be following.

It wasn't until mid-afternoon that she finally risked guiding them downwards.

"What is this place?" the paper butterfly wept.

Waves of heat rose from the parched ground, rippling the world around her. Strange thickets of alien-looking plants with barbed bristles clung defensively together, and large pear-shaped prickly fruits lay haphazardly across the earth.

The paper butterfly gingerly landed on one of the trees. Its reddish-brown bark felt rough and scaly; its thorns scratched at her wings.

"I am so sorry," she continued, bowing her small head in shame.

The Child of the Moon and Daughter of the Sun settled beside their friend.

"Don't fret, I sense that many generations of monarchs have passed through here," the Child of the Moon replied tenderly. "These twisted trunks and formidable thorns may seem alien, but they are probably just the tree's way of surviving."

The paper butterfly was still not convinced.

"But how can any flower bloom in this dry land?" she implored.

"It doesn't look as if it has ever rained here. How will you both survive if you cannot find nectar?"

"Look at everything we have already overcome," the Child of the Moon encouraged. "We are not going to give up now!"

"Wise words," agreed the Daughter of the Sun. "Let's rest under the shade of this tree. Then, when the shadows lengthen and the ground cools, we can search for nectar."

So, like two leaves suspended from a branch of green, the Child of the Moon and Daughter of the Sun hung in the shade of the honey mesquite.

"Thank you," the paper butterfly whispered, looking at the tree again in a more positive light.

She gently caressed its gnarled finger-like branches. Somehow they reminded her of her Maker.

"You know," she sighed, "I have changed so much since you first created me. I doubt that you would recognize me now."

She paused to look closely at her wrinkled fibres.

"I expect you remember when these wings were silky smooth," she reminisced, "but see how they now ripple like the water when the breeze blows? I remember being terrified when the angry droplets of water smacked against them. Now, even though they are wrinkled, I feel thankful, for without the rain, I might never have taken refuge under the leaf and met my Child of the Moon's father."

The paper butterfly looked at the oil stains.

"I recently became covered in grime and dust when I was sucked into the depths of a metal monster's rumbling belly. It was a frightening experience, but it enabled me to warn my friends and lead them away from the monster's grinding teeth.

My wings have guided me safely through many more struggles. They are no longer as new and fresh as the day you made me, but what tales they now hold within their fibres and what love has filled my heart."

"And so it seems, the cycle begins again," muttered a voice beneath her.

Startled from her thoughts, the paper butterfly looked down.

Below her was an elderly-looking creature walking wearily along the dusty earth carrying a rather heavy-looking shell on his back. His old bones creaked as he moved, and his long neck and four stumpy legs seemed to be endowed with way too much skin.

"I have lived a long old life, and have watched many a battle-worn monarch like you fly past each fall," the elderly tortoise reminisced.

The paper butterfly felt she should explain that she wasn't actually a monarch, but before she could think of a reply that she thought wouldn't offend this gentle creature, he spoke again.

"When the milkweed re-grows each spring, I watch the monarchs dance in the sky and lay their eggs. It is such a beautiful sight! I see the new caterpillars hatch and grow, and then, after a few weeks, when the milkweed wilts from the heat, they transform into a new generation of butterflies and fly north."

He paused again as if to compose his thoughts.

"You know, I count my age by this passing of time and each Fall when the monarchs fly south, I know I am another year older."

The tortoise carefully plucked a fleshy purple fruit from a nearby cactus and savoured its watery juices. Then slowly he turned his wrinkled head skywards.

"Maybe it's just my old eyes playing tricks on me," he finally continued, "but I am sure I used to see many more monarchs flying across the skies above me than I can see now."

Suddenly, the paper butterfly felt the air around her begin to move. Above her, a kaleidoscope of butterflies filled the sky.

"Come fly, come fly," they called.

The paper butterfly lifted her wings to join them. The Child of the Moon and Daughter of the Sun sensed the same rhythmic pulsing and rose too.

They travelled until they reached a wide-open plain where grasses blossomed with plumes of pure sunlight and tiny yellow flower heads glowed proudly above them. Drawn by the promise of nectar, the monarchs floated eagerly down. Then, as evening melted into night, they bid thanks to the blooms and clustered together to rest under the shadows of a nearby ebony tree.

The paper butterfly glanced around the roost of sleeping butterflies. Their worn wings glowed faintly in the sultry night air.

“My dear Child of the Moon’s father was right,” she mused sleepily. “These monarch's wings, like my own, may no longer be as fresh as the day they eclosed, but they are still as beautiful and remind us that coping with adversity is simply part of life’s journey.”

And with that thought she, too, closed her eyes.

Chapter 16

Boom!

The paper butterfly woke up with a start.

Peering into the inky blackness of the night, she tried to figure out what had roused her. The air seemed tense, quivering against her wings, yet everything seemed just as it had been when she had fallen asleep a few hours ago.

She could make out the shadows of the monarchs hanging silently in the tree, shrouding its ebony branches in their soft orange glow. Then, as her eyes adjusted to the darkness, she noticed a different orange glimmer flickering in the distance.

"What is it?" she thought.

Suddenly, a silver string of light sliced through the clouds and with a deafening rumble of anger, it struck a nearby tree with its misshapen fingers. Sparks flew, and flames engulfed its branches. The sickly smell of scorched earth floated through the air.

She didn't have time to think; didn't allow herself to think. Adrenaline poured into her fibres.

"Fly!" she yelled.

Seconds later, with a light so blinding that it lit up the entire world around her, another terrifying crack of thunder rocked the sky; this one so powerful her whole body trembled under its force.

Like an aggressive wild animal, the angry fire leapt from branch to branch, turning the tree where they had hung only moments ago into a raging inferno.

Amongst the flames, several monarchs fought valiantly against the swirling eddies of an angry wind. The paper butterfly cried tears of despair, as some were thrown into the inferno below, but she knew she couldn't stop to mourn for them now.

The fire stung against her wings, burning little holes in her fibres. Thick black smoke choked her and made it hard to see.

Then, through the acrid smoke, a familiar voice called out.

"We are with you; we can do this!" exclaimed the Child of the Moon.

"But how?" yelled the terrified paper butterfly.

"Our only chance is to out-fly the fire," answered the Daughter of the Sun.

Staying low to avoid the choking smoke that filled the air, they frantically beat their wings. Yet as fast as they flew, the mischievous flames followed, jumping from bush to bush like vicious dogs snarling at their heels.

"The fire is too fast for us to out-fly it," cried the Child of the Moon in despair.

Another streak of lightning shot down from the sky.

CRACK!

"Stay away from the trees," screamed the paper butterfly as the whipping flames scorched one of her fragile paper wings.

They swerved just in time.

All around them was an impenetrable wall of fire.

"Oh, my dearest Maker, please help us!" the paper butterfly exclaimed.

A large drop of rain smacked against her wings.

The paper butterfly tumbled downwards.

"No, you will not throw me into the fire," she yelled angrily.

Another splash and another fell. Then the heavens burst open, and a torrent of rain cascaded down.

"As if we needed things to get any worse," cried the Daughter of the Sun in despair.

But as the increasingly heavy drops fell, the angry flames seemed to change their mood. Recoiling from the rain's cold touch, the fire fizzled and then leapt away, leaving behind open patches of charred earth.

"Look!" exclaimed the paper butterfly in amazement. "The flames are retreating."

"It seems they are afraid of the rain even more than us," remarked the Child of the Moon.

They frantically began to search for somewhere to hide from the increasingly thunderous precipitation, but the once spreading canopies of green were now nothing more than lifeless sticks of charcoal; the beautiful flower-filled grass plains, burnt sorrow and ash.

As much as they searched, there was not a leaf in sight to shelter under.

"The fire has taken everything!" they cried in desperation.

They huddled together inside a charred and limbless hollow trunk, but the burnt tree provided little protection against the angry torrent of rain which tore relentlessly at their wings. The paper butterfly knew they were in real danger for, without shelter, the monarchs would most certainly perish. She selflessly placed herself over them to offer some protection but realized it wasn't enough.

Suddenly, she knew what she must do.

"Shelter under me," she whispered as she began, ever so tenderly, to unfold one of the creases in her wing.

"What are you doing?" asked the Daughter of the Sun, quite alarmed.

"I cannot protect you all from this rain in the form I am in now," replied the paper butterfly, "but my maker created my wings with many intricate folds and creases. If I undo them and lay myself flat, I will be like a leaf, and I can shelter you both."

Carefully, fold by fold, the paper butterfly began to open herself up.

"After the rain, you will fold yourself back up, right?" the Child of the Moon asked with a tremble in his voice.

The paper butterfly shook her head, for with each flattening crease, she felt the world growing more distant.

"I do not think I can, my dearest Child of the Moon," she whispered.

"But how will I cope without you?" pleaded her dear friend as he watched the paper butterfly begin to unfold her second wing. "You have always been by my side, even when I was a tiny egg."

"You and the Daughter of the Sun have each other now," the paper butterfly replied tenderly.

As she continued to unfold, she noticed how the flowing river of water cleaned the soot and grime from her fibres. The paper butterfly could now clearly see all the intricate creases her maker had created. She remembered how she had felt when he had first made them. How carefully he had folded her, how much of his energy she had absorbed, and how she had wondered why he had created her.

"Do not be sad," she said tenderly as her Child of the Moon shed a tear. "When I was created, I often wondered what my purpose was, for I knew that a paper butterfly, however skillfully folded, could not become a real one. Now, I feel as if this may be the reason why I was made.

I have had a wonderful life with you, and have seen so much beauty on our journey, but my wings are too damaged to carry me further. If I lie flat and become a leaf of paper, my fibres can protect you both. Then, when the rain has ended, you will be able to continue your journey to the Oyamel fir forests in Mexico."

The Child of the Moon and Daughter of the Sun tenderly touched the paper butterfly.

"We will never forget you," they replied.

Content that her sacrifice would not be in vain, the paper butterfly continued to unfold herself.

"Guide and protect each other as you finish your journey," she whispered weakly to her beloved friends. "My spirit will be with you always, flying on your wings."

As she spoke, a small milkweed seed became dislodged from one of her creases. The paper butterfly watched as the river of water washed it gently onto the ground below her.

"Thank you," she sighed.

And then, with one final unfold, Life left her.

Epilogue

Long after the monarchs had flown south to their wintering grounds in the sacred fir forests of Mexico, the milkweed seed sprouted beside where the paper butterfly lay. It was the promise of new life, the welcome fresh new green of spring rising out of the scorched, rain-washed earth, like a phoenix rising through the ashes.

Then, one warm day when the milkweed was in full bloom, two elderly monarchs with tattered paper-thin wings spiralled down from the sky like two maple seeds falling to the earth.

"We are back," cried the Child of the Moon. "The sacred fir forests in Mexico were so beautiful. There were millions, maybe even a billion butterflies, over-wintering with us. Some of them had paper tags, too. We very much felt your presence there."

They stroked the paper butterfly's decaying fibres with their antennae, hoping that she also sensed their presence.

Eager to tell her about their adventure, the Child of the Moon then recounted their tale.

"The nights were cool, but not too cold," he began. "We all clustered in a small part of the forest reserve, painting the trees orange, and bending their branches under our collective weight.

Then, when the temperatures warmed, we opened our wings and flew in celebration, and the forests transformed into an orange wonderland. Our collective wings made a sound like gently falling rain. This sound reminded us so much of the sacrifice you made for us that we knew we had to return here to complete our circle of life.

The journey back has been difficult because we are old and our wings are tired, but once our final gift to this earth has been laid, we will be with you forever."

Then they rose into the air and danced in the warm spring sun one last time before slowly drifting down, arm in arm like feathers falling to the earth.

The Daughter of the Sun flew over to the milkweed beside where the paper butterfly lay. She carefully selected the tenderest leaf and laid her final gift to the earth on its underside.

"Protect and nurture this small treasure, dearest Paper Butterfly," she whispered lovingly.

Then, content that their destiny had finally been fulfilled, she and the Child of the Moon lay peacefully beside their friend.

For one truly magic moment, time stood still and the paper butterfly's spirit knew that their epic journey was complete. She also felt a sense of peace and wholeness knowing that her beloved Child of the Moon and Daughter of the Sun's souls would live on, and the cycle of life would begin again.

A tiny, creamy white pearl on the underside of the milkweed, hidden away from prying eyes...

About Ona Kingdon

B. Ed (Hons), CSPWC, TWSA, NWS

Ona was born in the UK and, as a young child, loved creating and illustrating stories with her grandmother. She pursued a career as a teacher of the Deaf and frequently used her love of drawing and storytelling while teaching.

After a 16-year career in education, Ona became a professional watercolour artist in 2011. She is an elected member of the Canadian Society of Painters in Water Colour and a signature member of the National Watercolor Society and the Transparent Watercolor Society of America. Ona was selected as one to watch by the Watercolor Artist Magazine in 2012. She has won numerous awards nationally and internationally and has had articles accompanying her artwork published in major magazines and art books worldwide.

Ona is passionate about the natural world and has raised and tagged monarch butterflies for many years. Her garden, in Richmond Hill, Ontario, is an official Monarch Waystation and a registered Canadian wildlife garden. Visitors describe it as a haven or oasis, a place of tranquillity and safety. To Ona, it is a source of inspiration. Whatever the season, you will find her photographing or sketching the animals that live in it or simply observing them and mulling over ideas for future stories or paintings.

Made in the USA
Middletown, DE
18 December 2024

67627527R00088